The ABC's of Ghost Hunting

A Beginner's Guide

DAVE R. OESTER

ISBN-13: 978-1503320079
ISBN-10: 1503320073

Published by
Dave Oester, DD, PhD, Reiki Master
Coyote Moon Publishing
Kingman, AZ 86409

DEDICATION

I dedicate this book to everyone who has a desire to know the truth about life after death. Ghosts are the evidence of our eternal nature of man. Death is a comma, not a period in our existence.

Other Books
By Dave & Sharon Oester

The Prophecy
The Dark Wizard
Pandora Key
Hollow Earth
Lost Nazi Gold
Lost Aztec Gold
The Curse!
Ghost Riders Of The
West
Ghostly Haunts Of The
East
Gettysburg Ghosts
Tao Of Ghost Hunting
Beyond The Twilight
Beyond Death
Ghosts Of Gettysburg
Exploring The Haunted
Southwest
Haunted Reality
Twilight Visitors
Living With Ghosts
Forbidden Knowledge
Restless Spirits Across
America
Ghost Hunting For
Beginners
EVP Handbook
Ghost Photography
Handbook
Magic Dimensions

Truth About Parallel
Dimensions
How To Become A Reiki
Master
How To Be A Ghost
Researcher
How To Be A
Paranormal Investigator
How To Be A
Paranormal Counselor
How To Become An
EVP Researcher
Ghostweb Journal
The Donner Party
Tragedy in the Sierra
Mountains
Ancient Indians of the
Southwest
Haunted America Speaks
My Adventure in a
Haunted House

Books By
Dave R. Oester

Living In A Haunted House
Certified Ghost Researcher Course
Dave's Yummy Cookbook
Understanding Death and Grief
Certified Paranormal Investigator
Awa Maru Treasure
Lost Egyptian Treasure
Noda, My Alien Spirt Guide
Internet Dating Scams
Lost Sun God Treasure
The Red Lake Mystery
The Rainbow Bridge

Table of Index

EQUIPMENT FOR GHOST HUNTING

Welcome to the ABC's of Ghost Hunting. This book was written for someone new in this exciting field of study. In the course of this book, I shall talk about the types of equipment and tools used in ghost hunting. The new ghost hunter should be *caveat emptor*, Latin for "Let the Buyer Beware," as the tools you see on the TV versions, from Geiger Counters, to carrying axes for protection, is about hype and not about reality. TV scriptwriters often come up with crazy and unrealistic tools for the ghost hunter. Ignore them, just Hollywood.

I am a Master Ghost Hunter with twenty-four years of experience and head of the huge International Ghost Hunters Society (IGHS) established in 1996. I have over 12,000 members worldwide. I have conducted over 1,500 field investigations at over 354 different sites and recorded over 5,200 ghost voices. I have evaluated over half a million suspect ghost photos. I have the expertise and I am sharing my knowledge with you the reader.

Since the dawn of time, man has wondered about the supernatural, why the sun comes up every morning, or why do we have a rainbow after it rains. As man evolved in science and in understanding of that science, certain phenomena occurred that were outside of mainstream explanations. Thus, the field of metaphysics was born. It dealt with that which was beyond the physical understanding. As science progresses, the understanding may be explained based on new insights acquired in science. Metaphysics was not meant to be beyond comprehension or beyond understanding.

Understanding what lies beyond death has troubled man since the first man stared up at the stars and wondered where he came from. Since that time, Man has come to fear death. His man-made religions offered much in the way of hope and little in the way of validation of that belief. Man's religion did little to comfort him when faced with the loss of a loved one. Man came to fear death as the final end and not embrace it as a new beginning.

Metaphysics suggested events could exist outside our understanding of classical physics. We could measure these metaphysical events with electronic equipment designed for specific functions, such as EMF fields, Static EM field and temperature deviation from ambient norms. As time progressed, we found that Quantum Mechanics explained much of what science could not explain through classical physics. The subatomic world held the key to understanding the weirdness of certain metaphysical phenomenon that had previously been considered supernatural.

Ghost researchers soon discovered that tangible physical changes occurred when paranormal events happened. First, we discovered that electromagnetic fields either altered, or disrupted when a supernatural event occurred. The detection of electrostatic energy fields during paranormal happenings suggested the spirits of the dead were in some way associated with the electromagnetic spectrum. Later research suggests that the spirits of the dead were like energy packets within the electromagnetic spectrum.

Second, the researchers correlated that temperature plummeted significantly whenever paranormal events occurred. Researchers and witnesses reported cold spots associated with ghostly events.

These cold spots ranged from 30 to 60-degree temperature drops were beyond the normal expected range of the ambient temperature.

Third, for many years' researchers suggested those ghostly apparitions could be photographed using infrared film. The IGHS experimented with infrared film and discovered that the film could record paranormal events, but the safety requirements for handling the film and the cost of developing and printing was steeper than most beginners might afford. The IGHS experimented with other film formats and found that the infrared film was not necessary and that regular Kodak Gold 200, 400 or 800 films were just as effective at recording these anomalies.

These physical distortions captured on film suggested that the spirits of the dead could be detected by applying scientific tools that were designed for measuring such physical anomalies as EMF fields and temperature increases or decreases. The IGHS employs the latest in scientific measuring equipment that can record changes in the geomagnetic, thermal, and infrared spectrums. These measuring devices are the state of the art pieces of equipment. We constantly investigate and test new pieces of equipment that might be of benefit to the ghost hunting community.

Before the IGHS, traditional ghost hunters did not share any information regarding their findings. Research was a closely guarded secret known only to a few. When the IGHS was formed, it was decided that all information would be shared with anyone who had an interest. The IGHS asked that each of its members also share their findings with the other members so all might benefit from each other's research. I still maintain this philosophy today. As one of the oldest, if not the oldest ghost hunting society on the Internet, I feel that this idea of not sharing discoveries and techniques is what is keeping the traditional ghost hunters in the medieval period of ghost research.

Now, let me start with the basic ghost hunting black bag. This can be very basic when first starting. The basic tool kit for any ghost researcher should always start with a camera, compass, notepad, pencil, flashlight, spare batteries, and tape recorder with new tape. Today, the camera is normally a high resolution digital camera and the tape recorder is now a digital voice recorder. I will talk about the film camera for those who still use them, but most new ghost hunters will use a digital camera for faster access to their photos

CAMERAS

Film Cameras:

Any kind of film camera will work as long as it has a flash. We have used 35mm, the new APS cameras, and finally digital cameras with amazing results. We have posted photos on our web site taken with point and shoot 35 mm cameras, 110, 220, digital and Polaroid's. The camera does not have to be expensive, even simple disposable cameras have produced excellent ghostly anomalies. Special Infrared or parallel lens cameras are not necessary and the film is more costly to develop and to process. Ghost Photography is entirely different than conventional photography. Expensive cameras with plenty of bells and whistles are less desirable than the simply point and shoot cameras. We recommend that the camera has a good flash and does not require manual focusing.

Digital cameras:

The IGHS was the first ghost research organization to endorse the use of digital cameras in field investigations starting in 1996. At that time other ghost clubs were negative about the advantages of using digital over film format cameras. I promoted digital cameras because I felt that the digital technology was here to stay and that the digital media was excellent for capturing ghostly anomalies. The cost savings over film purchased and film developing paid for the digital camera in no time.

Digital cameras allow the image to be viewable immediately after snapping the picture. A digital camera is a good way of alerting others as to where the ghostly anomalies are positioned because you can immediately view the photo and see the paranormal anomalies.

However the downside to digital cameras are that they are prone to capturing airborne dust particles, including pollen and moisture droplets especially during the summer months when dust and pollen are the worst. Always test the environment first for airborne particles by shining a million-candle power spot light into the air and observe if any airborne particles are in the beam of light. If so, do not use the digital camera. The digital camera should have a powerful built in flash. When the flash is discharged and the ghost hunter sees sparkles in front of the camera with his own eyes, then this is clearly airborne dust particles being illuminated by the flash. These airborne dust particles will show up as multiple round orbs in the photo.

The digital camera is one of the best tools to evaluate a potential haunted site to determine spirit activity. Digital now has better resolution than conventional film cameras. Very seldom is the digital camera used exclusively, most often the digital is employed with other kinds and types of ghost hunting tools.

Any brand of digital camera will do a wonderful job of capturing paranormal anomalies. Be aware that most digital cameras set for twilight photos employ Slow Shutter, which requires a tripod mounted camera for stability.

Simply holding the camera in your hands will cause camera shakes resulting in photos containing light sources to contain multiple jagged bright lines spread across the picture. Do not use a 640x480 digital camera as its resolution is too low to properly evaluate photos. I would recommend purchasing the highest resolution digital camera that you can afford.

In the past, there has been much debate about the effectiveness of digital cameras. Critics claim that the digital technology is unproven and that it lacks the quality of photographic prints. Critics claim that the digital is defective. This is a myth and has no factual basis. The digital format is a proven media used today by almost all professional photographers. The quality of an image produced by a digital camera is now equal to or better than the film prints. These high-resolution digital cameras are affordable for the consumer and each year better and higher resolution digitals are hitting the market.

The new ghost hunter need to treat the ghosts as they would treat someone in your peer group or family. I suggest talking to them before taking photographs, introduce yourself and state why you want to document their existence. Why should the spirits speak to you? Do not judge or condemn them. Ask permission to photograph their presence to document life after death.

Everyone is a skeptic until he or she has his or her day of awakening. I do not look down on skeptics because I know they lack the knowledge and experience to understand what is happening as evident by the ghost photos posted. If you investigate with your mind filled with doubt, you will not be successful. Your doubts act like a beacon sending out energy messages declaring you do not believe that spirits exist. The spirit seems to interface best when the mind is open and free of doubt. Doubt is like a wall that prevents the investigator from obtaining anomalous photos of spheres.

Analog Video Cameras:

The Super VHS-C, VHS-C, VHS, or Hi-8 camcorders have all worked very well in capturing ghostly anomalies on video. The best analog video cameras are those that have night settings for filming at night. A built-in light is nice, but a regular external flashlight also works well. The camcorder should be placed on manual focus to avoid going out of focus and zooming in and out automatically. Place the camcorder on a tripod and focus on an object. Aim the external lights on the object, then simply walk away, and stand to one side talking. The ghostly anomalies will fly into the camera scan area and be recorded.

Sony has the 'Nightshot', which is a zero-lux infrared night vision camera that is a Hi-8 and digital format. Many of Sony's camcorders have this night vision feature so check them out. Panasonic also has a zero-lux setting for night time recordings. Do not use Super Nightshot as this is a Slow Shutter speed and any movement will blur the images.

Digital Video Cameras:

The IGHS was the first ghost research organization to endorse the use of digital video cameras in field investigations. These digital video camcorders work especially well if editing is going to be done on a computer because there will be no generation loss in quality. The digital camera works best if it has a night setting. Follow the same procedures as you did for analog video camcorders.

When using any camcorders, avoid rapid movement when filming. A slower smooth turn is much more desirable. Turn your body, not the camera when you pan from side to side. Try to shoot from a tripod instead of holding the camera, as the tripod will give more stability than hand held. The quality of digital camcorders offers the consumer the opportunity to produce their own DVD video.

Any brand of digital camera will function well in the ghost hunting field. The most serious issue with the small hand held digital cameras are the camera shakes that occur due to hand holding the camera. Viewing the camera shake footage is much like being on a boat in the ocean with choppy waves. The viewer is tossed back and forth and it is difficult to see anything in the footage.

Game Cameras:

The new game cameras are digital with night vision and can be set up so that motion will trigger the shutter. These newer cameras are ideal in situations indoors where they can monitor hallways or stairs when activity has been noted in the past. They can also be used outdoor to monitor areas that have had reports of hauntings. Only motion will trigger the shutter, so unless wildlife crosses the path, any ghostly visitors moving in front of the camera sensor will trigger the shutter and be recorded.

Wireless Surveillance:

Wireless cameras can be set up that transmit to a laptop computer or whose signal can be recorded onto VHS recording tape. The disadvantage is that for each hour of recording requires at least an hour to watch and listen to the tape. In the past video surveillance cameras were hardwired, meaning cables ran from the camera to the monitor creating a mess of cables to set up and take down, but now with the advent of wireless surveillance cameras the home owner can have multiple camera sending their images in real time.

Film:

If you do want to use a film camera then I recommend the Kodak Gold 200, 400 and 800 speed films and the same speed for ASP. I have photos posted on our web site with all ranges of film speed and brands of film. Remember the specification will vary between different brands of film so if one brand does not work well, try a different brand. Film has natural restrictions due to the physical properties of the film and so two different brands of film may see ghostly anomalies differently, one may not recognize the ghostly anomaly while the other film may record it fine. The Kodak films are sensitive toward the red end of the spectrum and the Fuji is sensitive toward the green end of the spectrum. The red end of the spectrum is where most ghostly anomalies will be captured.

.

EMF AND EM METERS

Compass:

The compass is the most basic form of a ghost detector for detecting changes in the electromagnetic fields. Watch for deviations off magnetic north to point in the direction of the ghostly anomaly. The deviations should be at least twenty degrees or more to be valid. Compasses are not affected by electromagnetic fields, such as power lines and other man-made devices in homes. Compasses are more effective than using the LED lights offered as inexpensive EMF meters. Avoid using LED meters as they are flawed and provide false information. These inexpensive LED meters are limited in range and the ghost hunter would not know if he or she is picking up man-made sources such as a power line or if it is coming from the presence of a ghost. Most LED meters will record from one to ten milligauss and this is too limiting to be effective.

EMF Meter:

The electromagnetic field meter detects changes in the electromagnetic fields, both natural and supernatural. It has been our experience that when the spirits of the dead are present, the EMF fields should spike between two and seven milligauss. Normal background levels are from .1-1.0 milligauss. This unit must be passed through the energy anomaly to be detected by the EMF meter. The EMF meter must be swept from side to side and from top to bottom to locate any anomalous energy fields. Readings beyond the 7.0-milligauss are usually generated from man-made sources and should be ignored. Man-made readings can exceed 100 milligauss.

The less expensive EMF meters that rely upon LED lights are not suitable for this kind of work. Inexpensive EMF meters may be attractive because of price, but their performance suffers and in the long run, the research will suffer. Invest in a good digital meter that allows you to see how high the readings are so you can consider whether manmade EM fields are involved.

First, determine the normal background levels outside the place the site to be investigated. Walk around the site to determine if any power or junction electrical boxes are attached to the site. Look for the obvious and eliminate anything that can be explained. Once a ghostly anomaly is detected, we suggest that photographs be taken of this area. An EMF meter capable of reading up to 200-milligauss is desirable to determine if the EMF is man-made and how dangerous to human health it might be based on how high the reading.

TriField Natural EM Meter:

This meter is most often demonstrated improperly on television where people walk around with the EM meter in their hands. Walking with this meter provides false readings. It must remain stationary with no movement by anyone around it. When used properly, it is effective to operate both as a motion sensor and as a monitor of the static magnetic and electrical energy fields. Watch for increases in these fields that may trigger a possible paranormal event. This meter also can detect the geomagnetic energy generated from thunderstorms and other electrical disturbances.

Home Brew Magnetic Field Ghost Detector:

Designed by Dr. Dave Oester, this home brew ghost detector can only detect magnetic fields. The advantage is that most electrical fields are man-made and not of a paranormal origin. No false readings will trigger the unit, as it is not sensitive to man-made electric fields.

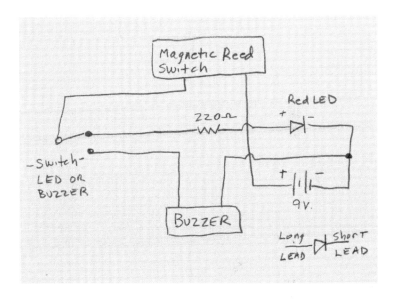

Theory:

When the magnetic reed switch sensor senses a magnetic field, the switch is activated and a circuit is closed sounding either a buzzer or turning a LED to the on position. The SPDT switch allows either the LED or the Buzzer to be active. Ghosts generated a magnetic field of between 1.5 to 7 milligauss and will trigger the unit sensor.

Construction:

The Magnetic Field Ghost Detector is constructed using basic Radio Shack parts and a special magnetic reed sensor manufactured by GC Switch. The GC Switch is carried by most wholesale electronic firms. If you have problems finding this switch, you can call either 1-800-938-1025 or 1-503-644-1025 and order it from Norvac Electronics. Construction time is about thirty minutes. Basic soldering skills needed.

The parts list follows:

1. SPDT level switch, Radio Shack #275-635a
2. 220 ohm ½ watt resistor, Radio Shack #271-1111
3. 12-Volt DC Mini Buzzer, Radio Shack #273-055a
4. Red Subminiature LED Indicator Lamps, Radio Shack #276-068a
5. Plastic Electronic Enclosure Box by PacTec model K-HM-9VB
6. Normally Open Magnetic Reed Switch SPST, GC Switch #35-750
7. 9-Volt Battery Cap

Placement of components:

I placed the LED on the top cover of the enclosure box by drilling a hole on the left side, one inch from the top and one inch in from the right hand side. Next drill a hole on the left side of the box for mounting the switch, just above the battery compartment. Attach the buzzer to the side of the battery compartment facing the top of the box. Any combination is acceptable for the spacing of the individual components.

Soldering Tips:
Use a low wattage solder gun or iron. I use a 15 Watt iron. Make sure the solder is fully liquid before removing the soldering iron. Allow it to cool without movement of component attached. Be careful to not apply heat too long on the LED leads as the heat will burn out the LED. The short lead of the LED is the Positive and the long lead is the negative that is attached to the 9-volt battery.

Testing:

Test this unit by passing a permanent magnet across the top magnetic sensors and test that the LED comes on. Next, change the switch and test the buzzer. If the unit passes these two tests, you are ready to begin using this unit for your ghost detector.

Purchasing EMF meters can be expensive so why not build a home brew unit and save a few bucks along the way. I created the circuit for the

Magnetic Field Ghost Detector and sold units through the Internet for a year before I elected to sell the plans only. All of the component parts can be purchased from Radio Shack, with the exception of the magnetic sensor. The telephone number of the magnetic sensor manufacture is provided or search the Internet for a GC Switch #35-750 . This is a basic unit without bells and whistles, but it does detect the presence of ghostly anomalies.

What is a Magnetic Field Detector? Typical EMF meters detect both magnetic and electric fields associated with the electromagnetic fields. EMF meters are fooled by electric fields caused by man-made or artificial sources while a magnetic field detector cannot sense the electrical field. The magnetic fields are responsive to paranormal anomalies and will not be fooled by man-made

.

THERMAL, MOTION, AND NIGHT VISION

Thermal Scanner:

This device is a digital thermometer that sends out an infrared beam that will bounce back when it hits a surface. The scanner will display the temperature of the surface that reflected the IR beam. Before beginning an investigation, determine the ambient temperature or average temperature of the area of said investigation. Sweep the thermal scanner from side to side and from top to bottom while viewing the digital display of temperatures.

Valid paranormal events will have a temperature drop that average between thirty and sixty degrees below the ambient temperature. Look for the icy cold spots and measure the temperature differential between the ambient temperatures outside the anomaly compared to the temperature inside the cold spot. Determine if the cold spots are moving about or if they are stationary.

Photograph the cold spots and surrounding areas. Temperature drops between ten and twenty degrees should be ignored. Do not point the thermal scanner at the sky, as the display reading is invalid. Outdoor readings may be flawed as air currents abound at different heights above the ground and therefore these air currents may give readings not associated with the paranormal, but common for weather related currents.

Infrared Night Vision:

I recommend using the second-generation models and avoid the less useful first generation. The night vision scope must have infrared capability or else an infrared lens must be acquired for your flashlight. The night vision enables the person viewing through the scope to observe ghostly anomalies floating or traveling in the air. Night vision is useful for providing immediate locations for ghostly anomalies that can be confirmed by photographing the area and confirming the presence by thermal scans or by EMF readings.

This Night Vision Scope is very sensitive and must not be used to view any daylight or artificial light sources at night or tiny pin-like holes will be burned into the lens of the Night Vision Scope. Avoid looking at someone when that person is using flash at night or potential burn holes may form in your night vision lens.

Flash is fatal when within nine to twelve feet from the Night Vision Scope. The Night Vision scope is used with thermal scanners, digital cameras, 35mm cameras and EMF meters to confirm the presence of ghostly anomalies that are called the spirits of the dead. Almost everyone who will see 'floating orbs" for the first time will comment that they look exactly the same as they do in the photos published at www.ghostweb.com.

Today, we does not use the Night Vision scope because the Sony Night Shot camcorder has a built-in night vision scope and enables recording of the images to occur. The Sony Night Shot Camcorders eliminated the need for individual night vision scopes and can record what is being observed, a drawback to just using the scope by itself.

Motion Sensor:

The motion sensor is an effective tool for sensing the movement of the spirits of the dead. Many IGHS researchers have confirmed sensors going off with photographic evidence of orbs of light being recorded. The typical arrangement is to use the motion sensor as an alert. When the sensor goes off, point your cameras in the direction the sensor is facing and snap your photographs. Apparently the spirits of the dead are moving so fast that we cannot see them or they are moving very slowly. However, they are not visible to our eyes but they can be detected with a motion sensor.

EVP RECORDERS

Digital & Tape Recorder:

EVP stands for Electronic Voice Phenomena and is the method of recording the voices of the dead with a digital recorder or onto audio tape usually done with a tape recorder or micro cassette recorder. The simplest method used by early ghost hunters were to use a tape recorder and a new blank tape that is inserted into the recorder.

If this method of recording ghost voices is used, then turn up the volume and start recording. The tape recorder may be placed in a room, on a gravestone or simply carried around with you while it is recording. The tape recorder is not sensitive to dust bunnies, which makes it an ideal tool for the summer months.

Any brand of tape recorder will work at recording EVP. Basic Radio Shack tape recorders work very well. I recommend using the most inexpensive audio tapes designed for voices. There is no need for high CD quality tapes for recording EVP because generally only voices will be recorded, not concerts.

I have used the 60-minute tapes, with thirty minutes on each side. Digital recorders work very well and this is my choice for recording EVP. I recommend using any brand digital recorder. Any digital recorder will work as long as there is no digital static being recorded. Digital static sounds like screams and demonic curses and fooled many people who used the first generation Panasonic Recorder when it first came out. Always avoid first generation digital recorder as they often picked up internal IC static noise.

Acoustica and Adobe Audition Software:

We use a shareware software called Acoustica 2.25 to edit and remove background noise when I evaluate the EVP. Your friendly search engine should find this shareware for you. Adobe Audition 1.5 is a product of Adobe Systems Incorporated at www.adobe.com. Acoustica 2.25 is shareware software that can be found by using a search engine. The software comes from Germany and can be downloaded and purchased for about USD $15.

EVP Recording:

When recording for EVP, it is okay to talk in a normal voice and to move around. External microphones will remove the noise generated by the older tape recorder gears. The key is to know the people you are talking to and can identify their voices so when you listen to the tape, you can automatically eliminate those voices you recognize.

Directional microphones and directional amplified microphones are also excellent for weak EVP voices. Some directional amplified microphones will use a parabolic dish. The important thing to remember is to invite the spirits to leave a message on the recording tape.

Some people will place the voice recorder on a stationary object and walk away, leaving the tape recorder recording. Successful EVP has been accomplished with standard hand-held voice recorders, including cell phones and baby monitors.

I do not recommend using the Voice Activated mode, but continuous recording. I have found my greatest success comes from recording for about two minutes at each site location. I then move to another site and record for other one or two minutes on a new track if using a digital recorder. I found that almost all of my EVP came within the first one or two minutes after I start recording, so now I developed the protocols for recordings in two-minute tracks.

Voices of the dead are recorded from 350 hertz to about 1,350 hertz. The range for the human ear starts at about 250 for tones, but many people cannot hear words at this low frequency. If we still our minds and silence the mental chatter, we would have a better opportunity for hearing these voices. It does not take special equipment to do EVP as some suggest. I have proven that any tape or digital recorder will work.

Never reuse the tapes, always use a new one to avoid possible orphan sounds and voices not erased on the old tape. Skeptics love to suggest that EVP be actually previous conversations that were not erased from the audio tape. We recommend using audio tape designed for voice, which is usually the least expensive tape. We use sixty-minute audio tape for our field investigations.

Digital tape recorders are giving amazing results with recording the voices of the dead. The digital format eliminates any concerns that the audio tape had previous recordings imprinted onto the tape.

Some digital recorders will record digital static so upon playback, high amplitude garbled sounds will be heard. Ignore the digital static and look for actual voices very near the threshold of sound. Current second generation digital recorders have eliminated the digital static that so many novices thought were demonic voices. Also note that ghost voices never are monotone, but are filled with emotions. The voice can be quiet as in a whisper or sound like the entity is standing right next to you.

Bionic Ear:

The bionic ear or directional amplified parabolic dish may seem like a good idea, but my experience using one was less than desirable. While the appearance of a parabolic dish may be impressive to outsiders, dedicated ghost researchers quickly realizes that these directional amplified parabolic dishes are no more effective than using an ordinary digital recorder with the built-in microphone.

Remember that ghosts do not have a human voice box so picking up audio voices of ghosts with a Bionic Ear is more hype from Hollywood.

A ghost hunter will record ghost voices with a voice recorder because the ghost is emitting electrical energy that the microphone would normally pick up as audio and convert it to electrical impulses, which is not need by the ghost. His voice is already in the electrical impulse mode and can be recorded directly to a magnetic tape or an IC chip.

Bottom Line:

After conducting field investigations for the past twenty-four years, I have come to the conclusion that the two most basic tools I use on a regular basis are a digital camera or digital camcorder and a digital voice recorder.

All of the other bells and whistles will fall by the wayside. While taking temperature readings, getting motion sensors alarms going off, watching digital meters move back and forth are all nice, but they provide no ongoing evidence that the investigator can take home with them after the investigation.

Photographs are two-dimensional so distance and size cannot be determined unless the anomaly is behind an object of known size and distance from the camera. The EVP ghost voice recorded can be listened to time and again. When the EVP segment is played human emotions are heard in the ghost voice or voices.

Geiger Counters, Gravity Meters, and other kinds of scientific tools are not effective. Ghosts are not radioactive nor do they register on a Gravity Meter. This is again hype by Hollywood.

WHAT ARE ORBS?

When I coined the term "orb" back in 1995 that appeared in our book, *Haunted Reality* published in 1996, it was to explain the shape of the balls of light that we captured with the digital camera and that a person could see with their human eye. It also described the shape of environmental anomalies such as moisture droplet, dust, and pollen particles floating in the air. An orb was not a noun, but an adjective that described the shape.

I had no idea that within eleven years, the term "orb" would mean a paranormal ghost, instead of a physical description of an anomaly, both natural and paranormal. Today hundreds of web sites have posted photos of multiple orbs and declared these photos to be valid ghost photos.

However, they are airborne dust particles known as dust orbs and not the wished for ghost orbs. Today orbs are as different as night is to day, on one side of the coin is the valid ghost or spirit orb, and on the flip side of the coin is the dust orb.

I created the Spirit Orb Theory based on the findings of our field investigations and through our research. I discovered that an orb or ball of light represented the soul of a departed person. The soul being the essence of who they were in life, complete with their intelligence, their emotions and their personality.

The soul represents everything we are in life except for the physical structure we call the body. The soul is the spirit. I do not separate the terms, soul, spirit or ghost, as they all represent the same spiritual entity. A ghost and a spirit are the same entity, just with different labels, nor do we attach significance regarding how they are document as in a level one or a level five event.

Ghosts are ghosts/spirits/souls and it is the living who attempts to segregate these spiritual entities into categories representing levels of manifestation. This is meaningless and provide no insights into the world of the dead. I teach that some souls anchor themselves to this earth plane because of unresolved issues or unfinished business. Souls not anchored to this earth plane can and do return to visit loved ones or friends, but are not haunting spirits, but simply spirits. The name is not important, it is only a label created by the living to identify the dead.

The shape of an orb or sphere is common to our everyday lives. Consider that the earth and moon are spheres, or that our blood cells are sphere shaped. We use the symbol of the circle to represent eternal existence, with no beginning or end.

I teach that a spirit represents an orb configuration or energy pattern. When the spirit is moving about, its shape is an orb with a contrail behind it, but when it comes to rest, meaning that it is no longer in motion, the spirit energy that is compressed within the orb is released and this spirit energy expands into what we call Ecto-Vapor or Ectoplasm.

The best evidence of a spirit orb is when it is in motion and leaving a contrail behind it. The contrail must be long, as rain droplets will leave a very small blur behind them. The reason for the long contrail is that the spirit entity is moving faster than the camera shutter speed.

I have discovered that a ghost orb is not always a single entity or soul, but it may contain multiple souls. I videotaped two floating orbs at Iverson's Pits on the Gettysburg battlefield, passing in front of trees and behind trees, disappearing completely and reappearing at a new location.

The two balls of light, one following the other reached the left side of the video frame and then each orb split into three separate orbs or balls of light, then merging back together as one orb. Hundreds of people at our ghost conference viewed this remarkable video the day after it was videotaped. This video is one of the best proofs that a single orb may contain one or more individual orbs.

This is the same video segment that Fox TV used and brought in a special effects expert who said the ghost lights were a result of smoke and mirrors because he could reproduce these ghost lights on his quarter-million dollar computer system. His statement implies that I had quarter-million dollar computer systems so I could fake our ghost lights. Skeptics are a dime a dozen, especially if being paid to be skeptical.

During the filming with Fox, they refused to interview anyone who was present the night we captured the Gettysburg Ghost Lights. However, Fox thought it perfectly all right to bring in "experts" who had no background in paranormal research and whose only purpose was to debunk my Gettysburg Ghost Lights.

He implied that we used smoke and mirrors to create the orbs because on his professional Special Effect software, he could duplicate it, but he showed no evidence that his statements were anything more than his theory. An important point is that his Specific Effects software is not available to the common consumer. To date, no one has reproduced the ghost lights on video with the use of expensive computer software.

Even in the time of Columbus, experts told him not to sail west as he would fall off the earth, back then the experts knew they lived on a flat earth with edges and beyond the edges were monsters.

Valid Ghost Photographs

In the mid-nineties, orbs were unknown and when seen with the human eye, these round shaped anomalies were labeled as balls of light. My late wife, Sharon Oester, captured this white vortex shaped anomaly on the stairs of an arts and crafts store in Scappoose, Oregon. She had just walked to the top of the stairs, turned, and snapped a photo with her 35 mm film camera. Nothing was visible on the stairs at the time.

It was not until she got the film developed that she noticed this strange anomaly. The vortex shaped spirit anomaly even cast a shadow onto the wall, suggesting that the spirit matter was solid and could reflect light.

I coined the term "vortex" to describe this kind of anomalous pattern, but later I dropped the term "vortex" and coined a new descriptive term, "Orb in Motion." This new term better described what we were photographing, an orb in motion that is leaving a contrail behind it.

The contrail will be brighter the closer to the actual head of the orb and will start to fade out at the other end of the contrail. Sharon's first ghost photo has appeared in national and international magazines.

An orb in motion should not be confused with moisture droplet that leaves a short contrail and generally, the orb tail is at a forty-five degree angle. Short pointed contrails are environmental and not paranormal in nature.

The below ghost photo taken by Sharon in a cemetery outside of Rainier Oregon. It shows an Ectoplasm or Spirit Energy that is floating near a tombstone. This kind of Ecto is different from the patterns formed by fog or smoke. Fog or smoke will appear in multiple frames, but ectoplasm generally shows up in one frame only.

A good indication that this is not fog is that it is almost completely contained within the photo. If a person walks through this ectoplasmic field, they will notice an immediate drop in temperature as if they are walking inside a walk-in freezer.

Ectoplasm next to a tombstone at the Rainier Cemetery taken with a film camera.

The next photo was taken at the Rainier Cemetery of a full body apparition that I call the Blue Lady. Sharon captured this in two different frames.

Airborne Dust, Pollen, Moisture, and Sand Orbs

Airborne environmental orbs are the most common anomalies mistaken for ghosts and for aliens. Amateur ghost researchers have created a new myth because they routinely label these environmental orbs as paranormal in origin.

Today, this myth explains that anything round and that appears on film or a digital image must be a ghost. This myth is flawed; no evidence exist that suggests that dust, pollen, moisture or sand spheres are related to anything other than environmental anomalies. This is a case where common sense is tossed out the window, but it is common sense that is one of the most important tools that a ghost researcher relies upon.

Almost anyone who purchases a digital camera will find he or she can successfully capture dozens of floating orbs in their backyard, in their garage, and in their homes. These floating orbs are environmental in nature and have nothing to do with the paranormal.

These dust orbs are very common and are the same dust orbs one wipes from the television screen or dusts off furniture. Dust orbs are not ghost orbs, but they do share a common characteristic. They are spheres and that is the only common factor shared between them. The most common mistake made by beginners relates to the size and position of the orbs.

The floating dust particle is near the camera lens and thus may appear to be either very large or over somebody's head. Since photographs are two-dimensional, distance and size cannot be determined. A good rule of thumb is that multiple orbs in a photograph are dust orbs. We have included an example of what dust orbs look like in a photograph.

Dust particles floating in front of a camera lens will show up as orbs in the photographs. These dust orbs will also appear as sparkles in front of the camera when the discharged flash strikes the airborne particles, illuminating the particles as the particles reflect the light from the flash. One good safeguard for taking photos at night is to shine a one-million candle power spot light into the air, if any floating orbs are observed in the beam of light, then these floating anomalies will show up as orbs in photos.

The floating anomalies suggest that flash photographs should not be attempted; I recommend that instead of using the camera that this would be a good time to employ your EVP recorder as the audio recorder is not influenced by dust orbs. One-million candlepower spotlights are available at Walmart stores for about ten dollars.

I recently read a book about Sedona, Arizona and its dimensional portals. The book presented photographic evidence that aliens were coming through these dimensional doorways. The proof presented were dozens of photos showing airborne dust particles or dust orbs! Yes, these folks thought dust orbs were alien life forms!

They even included photos of orbs in motions and of vortices captured during the Halloween season as evidence of alien life forms. Dust orbs are the single most confusing topic for non-photographers. While visiting Roswell, New Mexico UFO Museum, we discovered photos of dust orbs taken with digital cameras at 640x480-pixel resolution.

These low-resolution photos were of dust orbs and blown up revealing the uneven surface of the dust particle. The authors had no experience with photography nor had they attempted to establish any kind of base line for natural environmental anomalies. Far too many people jump to false conclusions when viewing these round or spheres shaped anomalies.

This is one of the biggest mistakes made by people who purchase their first digital camera. These novice photographers will go into their backyards and snap digital photos. Suddenly their digital images contain round spots that they cannot explain. They did not see these spots before snapping the photos.

However, airborne dust particles floating on air currents cannot see seen or felt. The air currents containing dust particles pass in front of the small camera lens as the shutter snaps a frame, recording spheres on the image. The person behind the camera may see sparkles in front of the camera floating in the air. These sparkles are the flash discharged illuminating the airborne dust particles floating in the air.

MYTH AND FOLKLORE
ABOUT GHOSTS

Folklore suggests that ghosts are disembodied spirits that are nothing more than fragments of emotions left behind after death. This fragment is without intelligence and without an awareness of itself. This is a belief that should have stayed in the medieval period of history because this concept lacks any scientific evidence. There are many myths that surround ghosts, some are from folklore of the local region, and others are from a lack of facts that led to hypothesis derived from an overly active imagination.

Consider the fairy myth that started with Jacob and Wilhelm Grimm in the early 1800s when these two brothers determined to preserve Germanic. Now we add the magical ingredients that transform common sense into myth reality. An example taken from a night photography session where flying insects are captured at night with flash will show white anomalies with wings. Some people are convinced that the wings of these insects are really the wings of fairies. When we eliminate the scientific approach and rely upon myths, folklore, or tradition, these flying insects become proof for the elusive airborne fairy or perhaps the modern day equivalence known as angels.

The promulgation of traditions and folklore occurred when authors repeated ghost tales in their books. Many writers and scriptwriters seeking new material rely heavily on ghost folklore originating from psychic visions, séances, superstitions, legends, and unrelated myths. Most ghost folklore beliefs stemmed from the early eighteenth and nineteenth century writers who used personal beliefs, psychic explanations, or their religious dogmas to explain ghosts.

One of the most common folklore stories is the story that focused around railroad tracks at Villamain and Shane intersection in San Antonio, Texas. According to the urban legend, a school bus carrying children stalled over those railroad tracks and a train crashed into the bus, killing all of the children.

The proof offered up by local people living in the area consists of supposedly ghost prints found on the trunks of vehicles stalled on those railroad tracks. They claim that if you park your vehicle on the tracks and set the gearshift to neural, ghostly children will push your vehicle off of the tracks. I have conducted several investigations at this landmark.

However, it was my conclusion that the handprints were from the oils of people's hands as they opened and closed their trunks. Putting baby power on the trunk often yield handprints, but common sense failed to override the excitement and passion of the moment. The railroad tracks sit on a slope and any vehicle parked above the tracks will roll down and across the railroad tracks due to the pull of gravity, not the pushing of ghost children.

Teenagers would line up for blocks to take their turn of coasting across the railroad tracks. The night I were there, the atmosphere was one compared to a giant party with honking of horns and loud chatter filled with laugher. The dry condition lent to an abundance of airborne dust particles that many captured as dust orbs and screamed that they had captured ghost children.

In the scientific community, folklore belongs with the fables and wives tales handed down from one generation to another. The serious ghost researcher will not rely upon folklore as facts, but will conduct investigations with scientific tools, obtain photographic and EVP documentation and then present their findings of paranormal activity based on evidence, not on myths and folklore.

Unfortunately, many hoaxes fool people because it supports their beliefs. Consider the Angel Hoax of the mid-Seventies. A religious sect decided to send the "Angle in the Cloud" photo to those who made contributions to their coffers. The photo were sent out to Christians showing what many contributors hoped to be Jesus Christ or an Angel in the clouds and was promoted as authentic evidence of divine intervention.

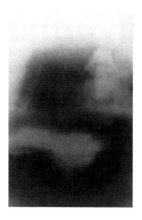

Many of these old photos ended up in shoeboxes filed away in dusty old attics and found by a descendant of the photographer years later. The story that surrounds the photo is always different, but usually it centers on some religious experience of the photographer, such as at a funeral services for a small girl killed by a drunken driver.

However, in none of the reported cases, have the negative ever turned up. The "Angel in the Cloud" photo has a long history; some descendants of the photographer reported it taken window of an airplane over South America, while other descendants reported it taken from an airplane over the friendly skies of Texas or North Carolina.

In none of the reported cases has the family member or photographer ever provided the proof, such as a negative. In all cases, the photographer is someone close to the family, a father or grandfather or mother who is no longer living. We still get reports today of this angel photo being taken by someone who just recently died. It is amazing how some hoaxes refuses to die.

In fact, the angel in the cloud photo was manipulated by the created by this religious sect to send when contributions were received. The photo was created for this purpose, to instill hope, and there by the contributor would send more money to them.

Another common hoax that floats around the Internet is a photo of an old hag standing next to an Asian youth in the woods. There is no explanation given in the email, but others have cut and pasted this old hag so she stands alone in a hospital hallway or in an alley or alone in the woods. Her feet are never visible, as she is floating in the air in all of the various versions of the Old Hag.

I started receiving my first copy of this hoax in 1998 and every year or two, someone sends us this photo thinking it is real. The Old Hag photo was just another case of myths and digital manipulation, yet some people believed these photos are real. The Asian youth was probably the hacker who photo manipulated these Old Hag images and once released onto the Internet, they now had a life of their own. Someone is always finding them and sending them to their friends.

The next Old Hag photo is perhaps the most common version being sent on the Internet. It shows the Old Hag in a hallway floating above the floor with hollow eyes and holding a doll.

Consider the Amityville House and the film called The Amityville Horror. It has been established that this demonic haunting was a hoax instituted by the owner and by the two demonologists ghost hunters who may or may not have been duped, but who went along with the haunting.

However, the demonic activity was a hoax to sell the story to the film industry. This was a typical haunting; a normal non-violent haunting, but the owners turned the events into saleable material for Hollywood, for financial gain. During the early 1900s, some unethical Spiritual Mediums or Psychics have promoted their products or sold their services to the general public, often to dupe the elderly out of their life savings.

These unethical charlatans employed hoaxes and other fraudulent practices to deceive the public, often employing spirit photography as proof of their claims. Later the Spiritualist movement began and fake ghost photography became very common. Often because leaders wanted to provide proof of their religious teaching so they helped the spirits along the way by double exposures and rigged photos, to provide proof of their claims.

Another common practice that developed during this time was the labeling of any paranormal event as being poltergeist activity if it involved moving objects. This practice misled many people in the study of the paranormal. Poltergeist is a German word meaning 'noisy ghost' and applies to such events as footsteps, knocking, voices, or anything heard, but not seen.

As some children enter their teenage years, they are prone to exhibit psychokinetic outbursts mislabeled as poltergeist activity by parapsychologists. A psychokinetic phenomenon is not associated with the spirits of the dead and has no place in the study of ghosts. Those researchers who explain hauntings as psychokinetic should never have suggested that the event was even a haunting. A haunting is an event that is associated with a spirit of the dead and not a psychic event.

This is a common yet little known medical sleep disorder that affects people. The person is asleep and suddenly they find themselves awakened by something pressing down on their chests, obstructing their normal breathing. The now awakened person fights for his life while fighting this pressure on their chest or around their throat. Most often, the victim will believe that this experience was a demonic presence with evil intention. Many think that they are being tormented by aliens. However, it is all in their minds, Sleep Paralysis is real and many people suffer from it.

Often the person experiencing this disorder sees a black figure standing next to them. This sleep disorder is very common and described in much the same manner each and every time. The more religious the person is, the more demonic the pressure is claimed to be. This is not related the spirits of the dead, but to a medical disorder. We have a chapter dedicated to this Sleep Disorder.

Another common myth is that EVP recordings of ghost voices are really running water that produce sounds that mimic human whispers and voices. While this sounds valid and scientific, the proof is entirely different from the theory. Ghost voices show emotions and any hypothetical voices from running water would not have this emotion attached to it. For example, EVP recordings occur where there is no running water. Most of the ghost towns and ancient Anasazi Indian ruins that we have recorded ghost voices have no running water.

These arid desert environments are void of any running water until a storm. We can also turn on the water tap and recording the running water, but alas no sounds like human whispers and voices are recorded by digital recorders. The running water myth may sound impressive, but it lacks any evidence to prove it.

Skeptics might suggest that it is running water under a castle that is haunted that is causing the human whispers or voices, but that is only a hypothesis that is not based on any scientific evidence. Where is the proof? The Running Water theory lacks creditability as we have proven that ghost voices display human emotions in their voices, which running water voices, if possible to record, lack.

Another myth about ghosts surrounds the concept of evil. Plato said, "No evil can happen to a good man, either in life or after death."

1 Plato argued that evil was merely the privation of good, that it had no ontological status of its own. Christian theologians such as St. Augustine and Thomas Aquinas were quick to accept Plato's position regarding evil, and lay spurious claim to his beliefs as if they were inherent in Christian theology.

2 St. Augustine said that the greatest evil is physical pain.

3 Augustine also said, "There is no possible source of evil except good."

4 St. Thomas Aquinas said, "Good can exist without evil, whereas evil cannot exist without good."

5 Evil takes on new meanings as we enter the twenty-first century.

Today we do not have Plato, St. Augustine, or St. Thomas Aquinas; we have television evangelical ministers pounding on the pulpit, screaming that if one does not follow the commandments of God, they are doomed to damnation in Hell. Evil is at their door constantly and if they stumble in their perseverance they will fall victim to Lucifer, the Christian deified god of evil. We are constantly reminded of human sinfulness, the presence of evil all around us, and the one method of salvation for souls destined for damnation. These are the same ministers with out-stretched hands seeking contributions for their ministry.

This mentality requires fear, shame, and guilt to be the primary factors in maintaining control over people. It is no wonder that any deviation in their surroundings and religious people leaped to the conclusion that Lucifer and his legions are after their souls. It does not matter that the change in their homes is a result of their own intense negative emotions because they blame the Devil, the father of all lies and contention. Passing the blame to something that is aligned with evil is easier than to acknowledge that they are their own source of negativity.

Television shows depict evil running rampant in our society; Hollywood generates films depicting evil as a diabolical entity void of love and compassion. This diabolical entity seeks the souls of the righteous and even those who are not righteous. We are influenced by the society we live within.

This influence is not judged with a balanced scale, which would indicate if one side of the scale was off balance. We tend to accept what we are told, be it truth or not and remain as sheep following a leader. We accept in our society that there is a lack of truth in advertising of a product, just as we know that just because the FDA has certified that a product is safe does not mean that every product is safe for everyone.

This is part of being "street smart" in our society, knowing that much of what we are told is not true yet is presented by those who are considered experts in their fields.

We need to be "street smart" when it comes to understanding about ghosts. If we toss aside the myths, folklore, and religious dogmas, we have a better opportunity to discover the truth for ourselves.

One of the first things to discard is the fear that ghosts are associated with evil. If the ghost that haunts your home is the spirit of your beloved grandmother, is she evil automatically? No, if your grandmother was kind and loving in life, she will be kind and loving as a ghost.

Ghosts are the mirror image of who they were in life, if they were happy campers they will be happy campers beyond the grave, conversely, if they were angry and mean in this life, they will continue to be angry and mean as ghosts. This does not mean that they are evil or demonic, only that they have a serious attitude problem!

Since most of the Western culture are members of a religious organization, who are taught that ghosts are evil and as such they are demonic emerging from the fire and brimstone pits of hell. It is interesting that most people have so little understanding about the language translations that generated the Bible. Consider in the King James Version the word "hell" is rendered from sheol' 31 times and from hades 10 times.

This version is not consistent, however, since sheol' is also translated 31 times "grave and 3 times "pit."6 The word sheol' was translated equally between hell and grave, we might suggest that instead of a place called hell, the term might equally apply to the condition when we are in the grave. It is easy to see how sheol' was mistranslated resulting in the term hell. So many translation errors have been made that now those errors are the gospel, absolute, set in cement, no questions and God has spoken!

However, common sense suggests that this bias and narrow-minded viewpoint do not represent facts, but are mistranslations of Biblical text. In reality, instead of telling someone that he or she is going to hell, the actual meaning might be that the person is going to the grave, as is going to die. The removal of the term hell that modern day religionists associate with damnation somehow takes the fear of damnation out of the equation! Without damnation, where is the power of organized religion? The three controlling elements are gone, fear, shame, and guilt.

The myths' spurious explanation is that God has cursed these spirits of the dead. This belief focuses on the myth that if a person believed in God when he or she was alive, then he or she will continue to believe in God when they pass beyond the grave, therefore the dead do not speak of God so they must be evil. Death is a mirror image of life, but without the need for religion and ceremonial rituals created by man for man.

It has been my experience that the spirits of the dead do not practice any kind of religion or religious rituals on the other side of the grave. Even Christian monks and priests continue to haunt their monasteries or parish home when they cross over to the other side. If deceased religious ministers haunt their former abodes, does this not suggest something is fallacious in paradise?

Religious people tend to believe that evil is present if negative experiences occur within their home. We have determined that in homes where negativity abounds, such as families where parents scream at their children and the children scream back, or where the home is experiencing stress from problems relating to money, marriage, jobs or other situations will draws to their home angry spirits with attitude problems of like nature.

The living blames the unrest and bickering on evil spirits tempting them from God's path. However, the negative emotions in the home are acting like a beacon that is attracting angry spirits. Misery loves misery and angry spirits seek out angry people to be around. Religionists label these angry ghosts as demons, but the ghosts simply are expressing an attitude problem in common with the emotional problems of the living. If we know people in life who are angry then they will be the angry spirits when they cross over, as we take with us our emotions and personalities to the other side.

We live in an age when Hollywood produces films that promote the concept that ghosts are evil and demonic. We do not realize that Hollywood has no intention of educating the public, but their objective is to entertain us with imaginary tales conceived by scriptwriters. In these Hollywood tales, scriptwriters have added gore and blood that is associated with evil ghosts, thus giving ghosts a bad rap.

Most films released will portray ghosts as evil or vengeful and that the living should fear these ethereal entities. Typical archetype has demons fighting for the souls of the living, portraying ghosts as demented or fragmented souls, often expressed as disfigured with horrible faces.

In the mind of the scriptwriter, the more horrible the ghostly face the more is the enhanced reaction by the audience. Thus, movies are made from what the public wants to see, and for entertainment.

As a professional ghost hunter, I have never encountered these kinds of ghosts in over twenty-four years of research and after conducting over 1,500 case field investigations at over 356 different sites. The ghosts I have observed have been human in appearance without disfigurement or horrible faces. Yes, some ghosts had attitude problems, but these were few in number compared to the ghosts that had good attitudes.

I have recorded over 5,200 ghost voice recordings and have evaluated another 1,000 ghost voice recordings, and in none of those recordings have I heard the ghosts cry out in terrible pain or anguish. I have heard emotionally charged ghost voices crying out for help or for someone they are looking for, but never the voices that Hollywood would have us believe are out there.

Many ghosts are the spirits of deceased loved ones who are visiting those they love. Many times a spouse will pass over to the other side and wait for his or her loved one to join them in the afterlife. Love does survive the grave and I see many examples of this in my work.

Death is not a period, but a comma in life's journey. It is sad that the organized religions fail to accept the spirits of the dead as evidence of life after death. While ghosts do not confirm Pearly Gates or Streets of Gold in the Afterlife, they do provide strong evidence of the eternal nature of the human spirit.

Our lives do not end at death, but we evolve into another kind of life form, this time without a physical body. Let us not operate in fear, shame, or guilt, but instead let us understand that there is life after death and we take with us all of our emotional baggage we held onto on this side. Let us remove that garbage now and be happier both here and on the other side. Death is not to be feared, it is just another adventure beyond this life.

I can remember as a child when my parents use to say, "The Boogeyman will get you if you are not careful." I become scared of the darkness because I knew that the night held untold terror for me. I disliked camping because sleeping outdoors at night was a real challenge for me. When I watched the Creature from the Black Lagoon, I just knew that I had to be careful around any water.

I grew up on a farm with a wooded area. I remember walking home through the woods one evening from a friend's house I had to pass a stump with a projection that looked just like a fin from the Creature from the Black Lagoon. I remember that as I drew near this stump, my heart started to beat faster and I had to hurry past it with my eyes cast downward, or I just knew that I would see this limb start to move. I have come a long way from being afraid of the darkness to investigating cemeteries at night without using a flashlight. I learned in the Marine Corps later that night time can be your friend.

While I do not believe in the demon myth, I do believe in the existence of negative energy and this negative energy can be equated as pure evil. This evil is not associated with religious dogmas, but rather it represents negative energy that co-exists with positive energy. This is the Yin Yang of Energy. It is not a conscious energy pattern meaning it is not intelligent nor follows some evil plan to steal our souls. Negative energy is like flotsam adrift in the cosmic sea. It has no rudder to direct its flow, but may come ashore and attached itself to a place that then that place becomes associated with evil.

Evil is a funny word, it is a label attached to ghosts when their action is contrary to our belief system. It all boils down to our own belief system. If we remain open minded or whether we close our mind to the possibility of life after death that is contradictory from what we were taught in Sunday school.

In Gettysburg, someone had labeled the East Cavalry Field as an evil place because some ghost hunters had experienced some intense energy that they deemed to be negative. I investigated the claims and found no evil, no negative energy, but I did find some ghosts with attitude issues. There was no evil at this site, but the ghost hunters applied their own religious views and their fear of the unknown.

We take our fears with us into adult life. Now when I walk through a graveyard at night, I do not think about the Boogeyman or the Creature of the Black Lagoon, but I must admit that I do have an active mind and I do think about all of those horror movies that Sharon and I have watched in the past.

At night nothing, or I should say anyone will come out of the darkness to grab you or to rip your head from your body. Perhaps that is why I love to conduct EVP investigations during the day. No night work, no creatures lurking in the darkness waiting to welcome me to their feeding area, just in case I am wrong.

STANDARDS AND PROTOCOLS

The International Ghost Hunters Society is the largest ghost research organization on the Internet. The membership has always been free and they teach that all investigations should be free of charge to the public. They have developed a set of standards and protocols for conducting field investigations based on experience and common sense. These standards and protocols establish a baseline to judge evidence obtained by eliminating the common errors of most beginners.

- Ask the spirits of the dead for permission to take their photos or to record their voices.
- Respect posted property, ask permission, and do not trespass.
- Always conduct your investigations in a professional manner.
- Show reverence and respect in cemeteries, battlefields, historic sites, etc.
- No running or horse play in cemeteries or historical sites.

- Positive Mental Attitude is very important for all investigations
- Skeptical minds will generate negative energy during an investigation. Do not bring along skeptics or those who are negative or want proof that ghosts exist.
- Follow the lunar cycles and solar storms for conducting investigations for best results. The paranormal events occur during peak geomagnetic field conditions near the full and new moons.
- Do not take photographs during adverse weather conditions, such as rain, mist, fog, snow, windy, or dusty conditions.
- Take photos of dust particles, pollen, moisture droplets to see how your camera records these kinds of orbs.
- An orb is not special or unique. An orb is only a description of shape. Most common orbs are airborne dust particles. Multiple orbs in photos are almost always dust particles, never spirits.
- Do not take photos from moving vehicles on dusty roads.
- Do not take photos while walking on dusty roads.
- Remove all dust, spots, fingerprints from camera lens.
- Avoid shooting into the Sun for resulting lens flare.

- Avoid shooting with flash at reflective or shiny surfaces.
- Keep fingers away from the lens of the camera.
- Keep long hair away from the lens of the camera.
- Avoid shooting when foreign objects are floating near camera.
- Compare anomalous prints with negatives for confirmation.
- Flash is only good for 9-12 feet from camera so focus on that range.
- Always use fresh audio tapes for tape recordings.
- If digital, record in one or two minute tracks.
- After twenty minutes, the spirits will get bored, no need to record longer in one area.
- Do not rub the side of the recorder while recording nor walk while recording. Stand still to record.
- We do not consider Ouija boards, dowsing rods, pendants or séances to be valid investigation tools. They are to easily influenced by your own emotions.
- No smoking, drugs, or alcohol during an investigation.
- If someone is angry, that person should not be involved with an investigation. They will draw angry spirits and the other spirits will avoid them.

ABOUT THE AUTHOR

Dave Oester, DD., Ph.D., and Reiki Master is an ordain and licensed metaphysical minister focusing on the eternal nature of the Afterlife. Dr. Oester has worn many hats in his life. He owned an oil drilling company, worked as a treasure hunter, accountant, paralegal, and as the head of the International Ghost Hunters Society since 1996. He operates a small book publishing business called Coyote Moon Publishing. He has been writing books since 1992. Visit his web site at www.ghostweb.com. He now has fifty-eight books published. You can contact him at ghostsweb@ghotweb.com.

Printed in Great Britain
by Amazon